Where Am I Going?

BRIAN PECHAR

DEDICATION

I would like to dedicate this book to my dear friends and supports that include Joe, Kevin, Nick, Dan, James, Nevin, Greg, Maddie, Marlon, Miranda, Ansel, Ren, along with all of my amazing fans and loyal supporters from my previous book.

TABLE OF CONTENTS

Acknowledgements - i

The Disney Store – 3
Brother Ansel – 4-5
Is That Dave? - 6
Error - 7
The Holiday Party - 8
Giving Back - 9
Irony at its Finest - 10
Starbuck's - 11
Dan the Man – 12-15
Energy at its Finest - 16
The Newly Invented Nick – 17-18
Full Body or Else - 19
Off the Record – 20-21
Thank you, Rupert – 22-23
We Love Hillary – 24-25
Backstreet's Back (Always) – 26-31
The Upside-Down Bus - 32
Here I Come – 33-35
Two-~~Fitty~~ (Fifty) Pizza - 36
Queen Demi – 37-38
Pray to Saint Anthony - 39
The Selfie King – 40-41
Watch GTV Reality - 42
Soul Power Brothers - 43

ACKNOWLEDGMENTS

As an author, I get inspiration every day from the countless people I meet to the various, yet interesting experiences I have, to basically anything I encounter in my life. But, if you are reading this right, you ought to know, you are the inspiration of my writing and it enables me to enact in more ways in society to gain a great repertoire of stories for you the reader to read, of course. I love all of you readers from the bottom of my heart and thank you for your continued support!

The Disney Store

I was in New York City and I decided to check out the newly developed, Disney Store, which is located in Times Square. The second I walked in; I was amazed by all of the different Disney items that surround you inside the store and by the friendliness of each staff member working in the store.

I was browsing the store and a female worker asked if I needed help finding anything. I told her that I was just taking in the wonderful store and that it was my first time shopping there. She then brought a few other workers over to meet me and they were all very welcoming to me. They then loudly sang a song to everyone in the store about it being my first time ever at the Disney Store in Times Square. One of the girls then presented me with a certificate honoring my first time at the store and told me to have a "magical" day. When you're at the Disney Store, how can you not have a magical day?

I was so happy about getting a certificate and a song sang about my first time and experience at the Disney Store in Times Square. I then saw that all of the staff members had all different kinds of Disney character pins on their lanyards. I asked one of the workers if there was any way I could have one of the pins because I thought they were cool. They then gave me a pin of Woody from Toy Story, who is ironically one of my favorite Disney characters. They also said that only employees of the store are allowed to get the pins. I felt so honored when I received it considering I was not an employee of the well-known store.

From the hospitable workers to the certificate and pin that I received from the Disney Store, I couldn't have been happier on this day. It was truly more than just a "magical" day at this store.

Brother Ansel

When, you hear the actor's name, Ansel Elgort, you probably just relate his name as the guy who played Augustus Waters in the recent book-to-film movie, "The Fault in Our Stars." To me, he just isn't that, he is a talented DJ, superb actor, friend, and just a caring person towards anybody he meets.

Here I am with my friend and entertainer, Ansel Elgort in September 2014.

Since Ansel Elgort's career took off, I have started meeting him a lot in the New York City area and every time it is just a pleasure to see him. Ansel will always make sure to take pictures and sign autographs for every fan that comes out to meet him, no matter how many fans are there. He will usually take a selfie and a posed photograph with every fan, which is just beyond generous of him. He will also take the time to sign autographs for anyone who asks him and while also asking the individual's name to personalize it out to them. Not many celebrities will do this, but his great appreciation and time that he spends with the fans is just amazing to see. Ansel also has a way of telling which fans are friends with each other and who isn't. Ansel is able to pick up on it like he is psychic medium. The best part is when Ansel told everybody to always be friendly with one another. He then stated that everybody who is a fan and comes out to see him is one big combined happy family. Then, Ansel also goes on Twitter to always thank the fans that always come out to see him and expresses his love and compassion towards the fans. At the same token, he also follows many of his fans on Twitter, as well. The upcoming Hollywood star is just the best with his fans in so many ways.

The part of Ansel Elgort that not many know about is his stage and DJ name called, *Ansolo*. This is where he appears as a DJ at nightclubs and releases music under this artist name, as well. He has a lot of talent when he gets in the DJ booth and knows how to get the crowd fired up of excitement. At one of the New York City shows that he was in the DJ booth for, he saw me walk up to the booth and saw me while he gave me a big hug with such open arms. He said that he appreciates my support towards his multi-talented career. Then, a security guard for the venue tried kicking me out of the DJ booth because I had no wristband to be up there and Ansel told the guard, "He is fine and he is allowed to stay up here, as he pleases." This was just so kind of Ansel to do, as he went out of his way to stick up for me.

I honestly love and appreciate Ansel Elgort so much for his generosity towards so many people that he meets on a regular basis. Not many can compare to the kindness that Ansel shows to his fans, but it will guide him for a very successful journey and path for the rest of his career.

Ansel Elgort ✔
@AnselElgort

Back to New York on the red eye and the best fans in the world r there waiting to put a smile on my face. I'll always be appreciative 🖤

8:07 AM - 4 Oct 14 via Twitter for iPhone

Here is a tweet from Ansel Elgort dated October 4, 2014, referring to when I saw him with a small group of friends.

Is that Dave?

I was in Newark Airport, about to go through security to get to my terminal. As I was doing so, I looked in front of me and I saw the hall of fame baseball player, Dave Winfield, in front of me. I was completely shocked so I said, "Dave, is that you?" He looked back and said that he was shocked that I recognized him. He then got out of the security line to take a picture with me and I couldn't believe how tall he was in person. Dave then asked me where I was from and told me to enjoy my trip. I had a great flight because I was on such a high from meeting Dave Winfield beforehand.

Error

My friend John was on an entertainment store website that he enjoys browsing on occasion, as he found an error on one of their listings. One of the items listed, which valued at almost over three hundred dollars was listed for a whopping $0.00. That sounds like a deal to me. However, the following day, Alex called the owner of the company to tell him about the mistake. The owner was pleased to hear from Alex and couldn't believe that he made this phone call. Alex was then given a free gift certificate for the store and has kept a great relationship with the owner ever since.

The Holiday Party

I went to one of my favorite restaurants, Chipotle, in the midst of the Holiday season. They were aware that they were being placed in my first book, "A Day in the Life" so they asked me if I could attend their annual holiday party. Without a question, I decided to go because who would turn down that opportunity. On the same token, when the Chipotle staff invites you to their party, you get up and go to it.

I went to the Chipotle holiday party and everyone was so excited that I was in attendance. Some were shocked that I was there, as I was too. The party wound up being lots of fun as I was mingling with many of the Chipotle staff members who are always enjoyable to be around. I also was thrown off that there was no Chipotle food being offered, as they had catered food from the Cheesecake Factory instead. This food was absolutely delicious and I kept going back for seconds. The night rolled on and I had such an amazing time and I was so honored that I was invited to this party.

As the night came to a close, I had met this very nice woman who just started working at Chipotle that month of the party. Her name is Sherry, and you can only imagine how many times I have sung, "Sherry" by Frankie Valli, to her when I see her often at Chipotle. The funny thing about Sherry is that her daughter goes to school in Syracuse and also works at a Chipotle in the Syracuse area. It just seems to me that Chipotle is the rainbow connection for many families and friends.

Giving Back

It was a cold and chilly February evening in the Meatpacking District where both Nick and Joe Jonas were both working at a studio on their final album that the Jonas Brothers ever released in 2013. Both, Nick and Joe, went to have dinner at a restaurant called Pizzo-Teca, which has great Italian food. As, they were leaving the restaurant; a homeless man asking for money approached them. The both dug into their pockets to give the man as much as they had in their pockets. It was a very kind gesture on both Nick and Joe's part. Then, they both came over to see me and my friends to catch up with us. This happened very often between my friends and I with both Nick and Joe since they were always around in the city. After our interactions with both Nick and Joe, the homeless man asked us who they were. We told him that it was two of the Jonas Brothers and the man got so excited, as he jumped up and down in glee down the street. The great gesture on Nick and Joe's part was great, but when the homeless man discovered that it was two-thirds of the Jonas Brothers that had him out, that was just the highlight of it all for me.

Here I am photographed with both Joe and Nick Jonas dated back to June 2013.

Irony at its Finest

Peter Max did a book signing in Huntington and I unfortunately couldn't get to the signing in time. I was so bummed out about this because he had left already when I got there. So, I decided to go to Kashi with my friend, Greg to drown away our sadness of not being able to meet the famed pop artist.

I was eating in Kashi with my friend and out of the ordinary, a group of six people walked in the restaurant. Low and behold, Peter Max, was in that group of people and I couldn't believe it. So, as I was done eating my dinner, I went over to Peter to take a picture with him and he gladly did so. He also signed an autograph out to me as well, which was really cool. He also did the same for my friend Greg who was just as pumped about meeting Peter, as I was. He was very nice as he spoke with Greg and I for a few minutes.

I truly couldn't believe that this happened and I truly believe now that everything does happen for a reason.

Here I am photographed with famed artist, Peter Max, dated back to November 2013.

Starbuck's

I absolutely love getting a drink from Starbuck's on any given day. All of their drinks are beyond delicious and help brighten my day. I also enjoy sitting down in Starbuck's to relax and read. However a few years ago, I started seeing a middle aged man that went to Starbuck's everyday so I decided to talk to him. His name is Ram and he is from Turkey. I enjoy being around Ram a lot because he always has a good story to share. His stories vary from his experiences in Turkey to something he sees in Huntington. They are all highly interesting to hear about. One day, I asked Ram, "How is your everything?" Now every time he sees me, he always asks me, "How's is your everything?" I was blown away that he loved this modern question so much that he asks me it every time I see him now. I always enjoy talking to Ram and getting the chance to meet new people at Starbuck's. It is a great feeling when this happens as you enjoy one of their tasty drinks.

Dan the Man

Everybody can't forget a face or name like Daniel Radcliffe's, considering the tons of success he had for over 10 years with the Harry Potter film series. Aside from the work, he did in the Harry Potter films, he has really broke out into the scene acting and singing, yes I did say singing, in several theatrical productions featured on Broadway here in New York and at the West End in London. He has also been taking part in several different films that go from a range of biographical films to action films to love story films. But aside from the tons of talented work he had done over the years, I can now consider Dan a great friend of mine and I consider him to be one of the best people to make a fan's day on any given day of the week.

Here I am photographed with Daniel Radcliffe doing a comedic pose dated back to June 2014.

I have always been such a big fan of Daniel Radcliffe and had appreciated him and his countless pieces of work for years, as he has always been my favorite actor. For years, it had been a goal of mine to meet Dan and get a picture with him. At one point, I thought it would never happen because I had gone to see him in *How to Succeed in Business Without Really Trying*, over 20 times, but never had success of getting close to meeting him. It was such a struggle to task this goal of mine. Almost two years, after his 10-month stint in *How to Succeed in Business Without Really Trying*, he returned to the Broadway stage in the show, *The Cripple of Inishmaan*. I had found out where a press event was going on right before previews for the show had begun. I was the only one there as I was very nervous because I was just in the presence of Dan's seeing him get interviewed by several journalists. I was just getting so excited to meet Dan and it was just bound to happen very soon in that infinite moment. So Dan walked over to me and shook my hand while obliging to take a picture with me. A person that he was with offered to take my photo and my life goal was completed in that moment. It is by far my favorite posed picture that I have ever taken in my life. Then, I asked Dan if he could sign my memorabilia from *How to Succeed in Business Without Really Trying*. He told me that he had to run and do an interview, but told me that he would come back to me to do so in a moment. Five minutes went by and Dan was running up the stairs, as he saw me and said to me, "I promised to sign those for you, let me do that now." He was so pleased to meet me and was getting to know me at this time. He then apologized that he couldn't spend more time with me because he was busy doing interviews, but at the same token he was telling me all about his press day and about his upcoming theatrical role. He lastly took a selfie with me before going on to the next interview, and from all of this my life goal was completed, but just in such a wonderful way that I couldn't forget it.

As, Dan would take on Broadway for the third time in *The Cripple of Inishmaan*, I went to see the show quite a few times, but also went to meet and see him as often as I could. Dan was literally the best to me during this Broadway run and seeing him often was literally the best thing for me because it made me so happy and gave me something to look forward to for about four months. Dan would always take the time to sign all of my various items that I had collected of him for my collection. He would always gladly sign it and sometimes offered to take multiple items backstage to sign for me because he knew I had lots of different items related to Dan to have signed by him. Every time I saw him, he would always take my camera or phone and take the picture of us together most of the time. He would also do this with every person whom he met every time I saw him after the show. This helped everybody get a great picture with him and sent everyone home happily. For me, anytime I saw Dan was just amazing and left me always on such a high. But, the one moment I will never forget is when Dan lastly came over to me on my birthday and made me feel so special on my 21st birthday. It was the best birthday ever as he told the entire cast to wish me a happy birthday. Dan came over to me and signed my poster while writing, "To Brian: On your 21st birthday," accompanied by his John Hancock. When, *The Cripple of Inishmaan* ended, I was saddened because one of the highlights of many of my weeks were now coming to end with Dan departing from Broadway at the current moment.

Here I am photographed with Daniel Radcliffe dated back to April 2014.

By being around the Cort Theater to see Dan often, I got to meet and get to know many different people including Dan's driver named Felix, Dan's girlfriend named Erin, and my good friend, Ron. Felix is one of those guys who you always enjoy seeing because he never fails to give you a good laugh with his great sense of humor. The thing that I loved about Felix is that he put my first book in his car for Dan and other client that he drove to read. Because of this, Dan got to read my book with his girlfriend, Erin, in their car journeys together with Felix. When, I first saw Erin at random at the Cort Theater, she saw me and came over to me instantly knowing who I was and said that Dan said I am his biggest and most supportive fan that he has. She also mentioned how much Dan loved seeing me all the time in the city while he was on Broadway. Erin also stated how she has read my book and said it was an enjoyable read. This literally made me so happy and I was honored by these kind words. Then, through going to the Cort Theater often, I got to meet my good friend, Ron who joined me all the time there. The great thing about Ron is that he always says the funniest things. One night, when Dan was leaving the theater to meet the fans, there were these aggressive autograph hounds throwing hardcover books in his face to have Dan sign. Ron looked back and said, "What the hell is this, Holiday Inn, with these damn Bibles coming over me." Dan and I started cracking up because it was so hysterical and on point to what was going on at this moment of time.

Daniel Radcliffe has always been my favorite actor and the fact that I know him now and consider him a great friend of mine is beyond unreal. It's just so hard to believe how I went from struggling to meet him multiple times over three years ago and now it's as if I have known him for all that time. It was just great to see a life goal mine be accomplished, but done in a way that has made me feel very happy every time that I see Dan. I can't wait for Dan's upcoming projects to come out and I hope to catch him in the city one of these days, again.

Here I am photographed with Daniel Radcliffe dated back to June 2014.

Energy at its Finest

On a fall afternoon I was invited to attend a Cosmopolitan seminar at the New York Times Center in midtown. I was so excited for this event and it wound up being a fabulous day as I heard famed entertainers, Monique Coleman and Chelsea Krost speak. The two gave a brilliant presentation for Cosmopolitan, as I was completely wowed. As I was leaving the seminar, Yahoo was giving out free Jelly Beans, macaroons, and coffee that were all absolutely delicious. I couldn't even have dinner because I was stuffed from all of these appetizing items. The Yahoo staff had tons of positive energy to promote their latest application for different smart phones. Then, Microsoft was also there photographing people with the latest technological devices that they were offering. They were also giving out cool prizes for everyone to go home with. It was great to see how live and energetic both Yahoo and Microsoft was at this event. I truly had a blast this day.

The Newly Invented Nick

In October 2013, the Jonas Brothers announced that they were amicably splitting up as a band in a redirection to focus on their own individual projects. For the youngest and highly talented brother, Nick, that was a no-brainer to reinvent his career while doing some acting and embarking on a highly successful solo artist run. From the time when I saw Nick the day that he and his brothers announced their band breakup, he said about it that, "Things in life happen out of your hands that you have no control of, but we will all be doing things to still enact with our fan bases."

Nick Jonas, without a question, has taken that quote that he said to me and really put lots of hard work in to doing what he hoped to accomplish. The inspiring thing about Nick is his ability to stay perfectly well fit for any occasion, but primarily for his role of a mixed martial arts fighter in the new television show, "Kingdom." It is great to see someone like Nick Jonas influencing society to stay in top-notch shape and to make it a trend. Health and fitness are very fundamental in life. But aside from the fitness and training that he exemplifies, Nick has gone on to launch a brand new solo musical career where he is hitting all musical cylinders with his newest material. It is just impressive to see an artist truly transform themselves into a totally different artist while changing the ability to make music that will slide right onto the radio and various music channels while drawing bigger appeals every day. With this solo career, Nick has been touring across the country to promote his new music. The best part of this is that he actually wants to enact and have interactions with the people whom support his new material. He will hang out with fans before the show taking pictures and signing autographs, while playing a mixture of music in the background. In these meetings, he tries to spend as much time with each person as possible, which is just brilliant to see. Then, after his shows he also takes pictures and signs autographs, but the difference here is that he actually makes a toast and drinks with many fans after these shows. A lot of artists would probably jump right on their tour bus and leave the venue immediately after the show, but that's what stands out between Nick Jonas and many other artists. While promoting his new music and the most recent single, "Jealous," at the South Street Seaport, he debuted the music video there for his amazing song, "Jealous." Nick drew such a large crowd and went around trying to take pictures with everybody. Nick certainly tries to make time for his fans, while working very

17

hard with his new musical career. The intriguing part about Nick's new music is that I have been playing it for many friends and they all really enjoy it and say that he has so much talent under his belt. It's a no-brainer as to why Nick has been gaining enormous success from his solo musical career.

Here I am photographed with Nick Jonas dated back to September 2014.

With Nick Jonas taking off on a very high road, it is a road that will never stop for him and it will be amazing to see what things we see from the youngster in the future.

Full Body or Else

It was a warm summer night and I was waiting for the young and upcoming actor, Miles Teller, to leave a movie premiere. I saw him and shook his hand while asking him to take a picture with me. He agreed to do this and I handed my camera off to a girl to take my picture. I told the girl, "Take a full body picture because Miles is a great actor." Miles laughed and told the girl to make sure that she took a full body for me because that was what I had wanted. We took the picture and then I asked him to sign a baseball, he told me that he felt so accomplished in his young acting career to do so. As, Miles Teller seemed to be very down to Earth; I also took a selfie with him. He then told me to have a good night while thanking me for his support towards his acting. As, he was stepping into the car, he lastly told me that he loved the Mickey Mouse shirt that I was wearing. That was very cool to hear!

Here I am photographed with **Miles Teller** dated back to September 2014.

Off the Record

Following the Jonas Brothers band break-up in October 2013, each brother decided to task on several different ventures. But for Joe and Kevin Jonas, they got back together and went on a 3-date tour called "Off the Record," in June 2014 discussing their success as musical artists and the secrets of their careers that nobody knew about.

Here I am photographed with Joe and Kevin Jonas in Washington Square Park dated back to May 2014.

In preparation for the small tour, Joe and Kevin Jonas announced a scavenger hunt across New York City where they would tweet out clues as to where to meet them to obtain free tickets to their upcoming events. The boys tweeted out a very first clue that made it obvious that they were at the famed Washington Square Park. I got on a subway from midtown and there was a group of girls who beat me there and received the tickets. Oh well, there is always next time. As, I have a great friendship with both Joe and Kevin; I spoke to them for a little bit and got to catch up with them. They are always a pleasure to see. I was then filmed alongside Joe and Kevin's friend named Rob McClure who is a famed theater actor interviewed me for their segments to be used in their upcoming shows. Joe introduced me to Rob, which was very kind of him to do. Rob said that I was one of the nicest people that he has ever met and told me that I was one of the most supportive individuals towards both Joe and Kevin, as a supporter of all of their work for the past 10 years. Then, the day rolled on and I was in the city running several errands and I went to get food in Columbus Circle. I was leaving a food store in the area and walked past the Trump International Hotel where Joe and Kevin were filming segments for their shows, yet again. It was so random and I couldn't believe the irony of it. Joe, Kevin, and Rob were just as surprised, as I was. It just shows what a small world it is. But, the highlight of this encounter is when I saw Kevin Jonas see an inspiring musician playing music on the corner of Central Park West, as he then left a tip in his guitar case. Maybe that will be a spark to helping this young musician's career.

Here I am being shown in a video on the screen with moderator, Rob McClure being watch at the Off the Record show in June 2014 with Joe and Kevin Jonas watching.

A few weeks later, Joe and Kevin Jonas hit the road with their moderator and friend, Rob McClure for their "Off the Record" tour. However, unfortunately due to previous commitments and the inability to be able get to the venue, I had no way of possibly being at any of the shows. The inability part of not being able to get there made me very upset because I couldn't support these three friends of mine. However, many of my friends went to the show and said they had a blast. Even though, I was not in attendance, I still had a blast from the splendid receptions that the events were getting. However, the best part is that they used two segments from my interview with Rob for all three of their shows. I was told by many at the New Jersey show when the clips of me appeared, that they entire house went crazy and was screaming for me. That itself was an honor along with the usage of the interview I had done with Rob. Rob then mentioned that I was the "honorary fifth Jonas Brother," while that was such an amazing yet honorable compliments that I will never forget receiving. After the segments played in the New Jersey, Kevin asked the audience if I was in attendance. Mostly, everyone I knew that was there told Kevin that I wasn't. Rob, Kevin, and Joe were very shocked and saddened that I couldn't take part in the fun. They all wanted to know where I was and Joe told my friend to wish me his regards. The reception and responses from people about this night were just beyond amazing and it's a tale that I will never forget.

Joe, Kevin, and now Rob will always have a special place in my heart for their kindness, care, and appreciation towards others including myself.

Thank you, Rupert

Another entertainer who I had been hoping to meet for a long time since playing Ron Weasley in the Harry Potter films was Rupert Grint. Over three years since the release of the last Harry Potter film installment that goal was finally accomplished.

It was a warm, summer day, as Rupert Grint was leaving a press junket in Times Square where he told me that he would stop to meet me when he was leaving the event. Rupert kept his promise and came right over to me at ease. He was so nice and I told him how much he means to me as an actor and he couldn't stop thanking me for telling him this. He then agreed to take a picture with me, but he had his sunglasses on so I asked him to take them off for the photo. He laughed at that and took off the sunglasses without a problem. Then, he saw that I had two Harry Potter items and he willingly signed both of them for me even though a security guard told me I could only get one signed. He was so nice to me and really went out of his way to please me with the posed photograph and autographs.

I would go on to see Rupert a few more times while also seeing him in his Broadway debut in, *It's Only A Play,* where he does an amazing job on the theatrical stage. But, on one day I was walking through Shubert Alley and Rupert was just standing around with his friend and actor whom I also know in Connor Mac Neill. He recently starred in Broadway's *The Cripple of Inishmaan* alongside the other Harry Potter star, Daniel Radcliffe. The irony really does come out here. Rupert finally remembered me by my first name this time and told Connor to take my picture with him, as he also signed a few things for me in addition to that.

Here I am being photographed with Rupert Grint dated back to October 2014.

**Here I am being photographed with Rupert Grint
dated back to August 2014.**

Rupert Grint is truly one of the nicest celebrities that I have ever met who really does go the extra mile to meet all of his fans and give them each a pleasurable and memorable experience.

We Love Hillary

As I do my best to refrain from speaking about politics, I have to share how amazing and what a kind person that the political figure, Hillary Rodham Clinton is when you have the chance to meet her in person. She is a very talented writer, but is very good with accommodating time for the people who support her.

Here I am being photographed with Hillary Rodham Clinton dated back to August 2014.

In summer 2014, Hillary went on a book signing tour to promote her latest book, "Hard Choices." At this event, there were over a thousand people in attendance and Hillary Rodham Clinton ensured to meet each of the thousand plus people while having an interaction with each and every one of them. She would talk to each supporter about his or her life goals or anything that came to mind. No person that went up to Hillary left disappointed for such a large crowd that went out to meet her. Then, it was my chance to meet the First Lady herself, and I will admit that I was very nervous about doing so. Hillary greeted me with a warm hello and I told her about my admiration for her and she really did enjoy hearing that. However, due to her time constraints, Hillary was unable to take posed photographs with people at the signing. But, being persistent as I am, I asked her if I could quickly take a photo with her because she means a lot to me. She told me "I'm not really allowed to, but since you were so nice to me, I will." I had to grab my phone out of my hand and place it on the front-face camera setup. In the midst of doing so, a secret service person said to me, "Dude, she just said to take a picture with her, get it all ready man." With the support of both the Secret Service and Hillary, I was able to get a great photo with her and it was really a dream come true.

I always try to steer away from discussing politics or political figures for that matter, but having such a great encounter and meeting with Hillary Rodham Clinton was beyond mind-blowing and exciting. It truly was an encounter and a photograph that I will never forget obtaining.

Backstreet's Back (Always)

In 2012, all five original members of the Backstreet Boys, whom include; Nick Carter, AJ McLean, Brian Littrell, Howie Dorough, and Kevin Richardson, all came back together to create their latest album "In A World Like This" and embarked on doing lots of press and touring. On their most recent tours, I was able to see the band perform in the New York area at Jones Beach Theater, which was a night that I will never forget.

Here is a photograph that I took of all of the Backstreet Boys opening up their Jones Beach concert with their single, "The Call."

In August 2013, I was attending my first Backstreet Boys concert with all five original members in almost 8 years since Kevin Richardson departed the band for a while to pursue other interests. I was ecstatic about this evening because it was going to be the first time meeting four of the members aside from Nick Carter whom I had previously met. The weather held up at Jones Beach and I went to a sound check party where the Backstreet Boys played a few of their hit songs and also took requests from fans as to which songs to perform in this small sound check. And through the years, AJ McLean, was always my favorite Backstreet Boy whom I always idolized and whom I desperately wanted a picture with. AJ saw my camera and got off the stage to just take a picture with me. The picture came out beyond perfect. They then took the time to field in and answer as many questions from fans as they could even with their security edging them to get off stage for their next pre-concert ritual. In the midst of answering their last few questions, Howie saw me raising my hand and made sure to make the time to answer my question, which revolved around asking what was the hardest and most enjoyable part of getting all five original band members back together in over six years. Howie said that it was one of the best questions he had been asked all tour and the other guys also chimed into answering. Just from these few moments at the sound check party, I was having such a blast, and I hadn't even formally

Here I am photographed with all five members of the Backstreet Boys: Brian Littrell, Kevin Richardson, Nick Carter, AJ McLean, and Howie Dorough.

met them yet. Well, formally meeting all five members together was the next task of the day, which happened successfully to say the least. While waiting for this moment to happen, I was able to snap a selfie with Kevin Richardson, which was very cool. I went up to each member and thanked each of them for their wonderful music that they have created over the years. It meant a lot to me to tell them how much their music means to me while also having a big influence on my life. I then took a picture with all five of the Backstreet Boys, at last. Then, I asked them if we could do a picture where we all posed and did a salute, which referred to their opening segment of their song, "Everyone," on the 2001 Black and Blue tour. Talk about a throwback there

Here I am photographed with all Brian Littrell, Kevin Richardson, and Howie Dorough all in June 2014.

so Nick asked me if I wanted to do that pose at that moment, as I told him I did. He then, told his security guard to let me get a second picture on his own, which was beyond nice of him to do. The evening would roll on as they would play all of their newly released music and old hit songs at the actual concert. It was one of the best concerts I had attended in years. One thing that the Backstreet Boys do after most concerts is have an after party at the venue with many of their fans. It was a great ending to an amazing day and night of Backstreet adventures. At this after party, Nick was the house DJ, while Howie, AJ, and Kevin roamed around greeting fans and bringing some of them on to the small stage that they were consistently on throughout the night. However, Brian on the other hand was not in attendance because he was resting after his long concert day. I was able to tell them how awesome the show was and they enjoyed hearing that, as they all proceeded to take pictures with me to cap off the amazing night of Backstreet fun.

Here I am photographed with AJ McLean in June 2014.

About a month after this concert, I saw Nick Carter in New York City when he was doing a book signing for his debut book, "Facing the Music." The book is a great read as he writes about his previous struggles and tries to influence the reader on trying to being a better person every day and not letting anything get in the way of that. Nick's messages in the book were very inspiring and the book should be a must-read for all people. It's a great book. Anyways, I waited last to go up to Nick at his book signing, and I asked him if I could take a picture with him, even though time constraints wouldn't allow it. He remembered me at ease from previous times and told me that he would do so. He then had his security guard take the picture for me while he stood up and took a posed photograph with me. Then, Nick saw I had an item from his solo musical tour and offered to sign it for me without hesitation. It was great how Nick was going out of his way to be super kind and accommodating towards me. Later in the year, I was able to see Nick with his kind and beautiful wife, Lauren, whom he stars in a current reality show with. She was very kind to me and allowed me to take a picture with both her and Nick. Since then, she has remembered me and always gives me a warm hug and greeting every time she sees me. Lauren and Nick make a great marriage with the amount of kindness that they show each other and others. The same day, I met Lauren with Nick; I was on cloud nine when Nick Carter also happily followed me on Twitter.

Here I am photographed with Lauren and Nick Carter in September 2014.

Whether the Backstreet Boys are together or separately, they never fail to happily please their fans through many kind gestures. They are probably the most hospitable band around considering the great success that they have had going on for over 21 years. I look forward to many more great experiences, music, and partying with them for years to come.

The Upside-Down Bus

When you are walking in Times Square, you probably get annoyed of seeing all of these rappers trying to throw their CD's in your face or a touring company asking you to join their sightseeing tours. In this instance, a young man was promoting a New York City sightseeing tour, which took place on a large bus. He was using a large sized poster in order to do so. However, his advertising skills were not good at all, as his sign was flipped upside down and that's the way the bus appeared to be driving its passengers. A midtown cop went over to the man asking him if you make it out of the bus alive. The man seemed so confused, but the cop reiterated his statement by pointing out the sign featuring the bus facing upside down. I started cracking up hysterically and I told the young man that I think he should get into the roller coaster business if he wants automobiles to go upside down for any reason. When, I see these promoters in Times Square, I usually try to run away from them, but this time I am actually glad I stood around to have a comedic interaction with him alongside the kind cop.

Here I Come

One of my best friends named, Nevin who goes to college in Manhattan lives in the Baltimore area while he is on a break or not taking classes. For almost a year, he had been trying to convince me to come down to Maryland to join him for a weekend. I felt bad that I kept putting it off because it seemed like such a potentially fun and enjoyable trip. On a weekend in September, I managed to find the time to take this trip down to Maryland to hang out with him, see the wonderful sights in the area, and meet his kind and generous family.

Here I am photographed with my friend Nevin at the Baltimore Inner Harbor in September 2014.

It was a Friday night, when Nevin and I were scheduled to take a bus to go to Baltimore from midtown New York City. The bus was scheduled to leave at 6:00pm to head down to Baltimore. It was five minutes before that and Nevin was nowhere to be found, but at 5:58pm, I see him running down the block getting ready to hop on that bus to get away from the city. Hey, everybody needs to get away from the Big Apple at times. He made the bus and we were on our merry way. We arrived in Baltimore that night, as his parents came to pick us up. I met Mrs. Julie and Mr. Ross who were so kind to me from the moment I met them at that bus stop with Nevin. That night, Nevin's goal was to show me the area of the Baltimore Harbor, which amazed me by its tons of energy and beautiful surroundings overlooking the Harbor.

We went out to eat dinner at Bubba Gump Shrimp, which was beyond appetizing and it was just such a great dinner. Then, I continued to get such a wonderful tour of the Inner Harbor from Nevin and his family. The first night of this trip was a total success and was just so much fun.

1ˢᵗ **Photo: Here is a photograph I took of the White House in September 2014.**
2ⁿᵈ **Photo: Here I am photographed overlooking the Washington Monument in September 2014.**

Then, the following day, after a long night of exploring the Inner Harbor, we all slept in and rightly should have. This day started off as Nevin, Mrs. Julie, Mr. Ross, and I all went to Nevin's grandmother's house for a brunch with lots of his family members. His family was beyond hospitable and had the best food to eat at this brunch. It was a great brunch consisting of delicious food to say the least. His family took such a large interest in lots of my New York City experiences and tales, but mainly with the ones involving the Long Island Medium, Theresa Caputo whom they all absolutely love. I thought only people from Long Island were familiar with Theresa, but I was surely wrong about that. They were enthused to hear about my interactions with her previously and about the amount of support I have shown her in the past. It was an overall great time meeting Nevin's family and having a delicious meal. But, next on the bucket list was to check out the beautiful Washington D.C. I mean who doesn't want to check out the Nation's capital. At first, we headed to a venue where the famed actor and musician, Ansel Elgort, was heading for his concert in D.C. We met up with Ansel and had a great encounter with him as I introduced him to Nevin. Nevin was very excited about meeting and getting introduced to Ansel. Ansel was totally shocked to see me in D.C. meeting him and not in New York, as he called me his biggest and most loyalist fan that he has for meeting him there. It was great to see one of my favorite entertainers and friends on this trip, but it was pleasurable to do it with my best friend who got a thrill out of it. The best part is Ansel mentioned this instance in an interview that he did out in London. That was truly beyond honoring to hear. Off of that high, we checked out the Nation's capital while taking several pictures of the Lincoln Memorial, Ford's Theater, Washington Monument, White House, and The Capital. Seeing all of these historic landmarks in person was just truly humbling and exciting to take in. The night got even better and more memorable, as Nevin and I were just about to leave D.C. to go back to his home, we saw the motorcade for President Obama, which was just so fascinating and rare to ever see. This was truly exciting to witness.

Here I am photographed with Ansel Elgort in September 2014 in Washington D.C.

It was the last day of my trip to the Maryland area so Nevin decided he needed to cap it off for me with giving me a tour of the suburban areas of Towson, Maryland. The area just was so unique and different from any town I have been to in the New York area. These towns were truly the definition of what a suburban town is and it reminded me of going down Wisteria Lane in the great television series, Desperate Housewives. The tour was so much fun as we were blasting everything from the current hit song, "Jealous" by Nick Jonas to all different hip hop and oldie songs. However, I don't think our musical choices would fit properly into a DJ set. The most amazing part of this tour was that Nevin was driving me around in a stick shift car, which was just so fascinating to see.

I am beyond blessed and grateful that I finally made the time and effort to join Nevin and his kind family in the Maryland area. Everybody that I met truly went out of his or her way to make me feel welcomed and at home, which was just so dignifying to me. Also, seeing Ansel Elgort on this trip was probably the icing on the cake for this trip. It was beyond amazing and I would totally make this trip happen again.

Two-~~Fitty~~ (Fifty) Pizza

Every Tuesday night in the summer, the Northport village always hosts a fair consisting of different delicious foods, street vendors, and vintage cars. It is a fun time no matter which Tuesday evening you attend. This one instance, there was a food vendor selling slices of cheese pizza, which appeared to seem very fresh and delicious. Usually, pizza gives me a typical craving, but in this instance, this craving just urged me to run over and grab a slice. I asked the vendor how much the slice of pizza was and he replied saying, "Two-fitty like out from my origin in Brooklyn." This was just so funny to hear and I couldn't stop laughing, but the best part here is how he linked together delicious pizza and connected with his growing roots derived from Brooklyn. I just wonder if I will cross paths again with this comedic pizza vendor in either Northport or Brooklyn. That is just a burning question that I have.

Queen Demi

Over the years, I have grown a strong passion of love and support for the highly talented entertainer, Demi Lovato. She is one of the sweetest yet most inspiring people that you will ever meet or see.

Back in June 2014, I was waiting outside of an event in Harlem in hopes of getting a picture with Demi Lovato. So, there were about fifty other people hoping to get the same thing that I had wanted, I mean who wouldn't want their photograph taken with the multi-talented artist. Demi's car pulls up and the five security guards working outside of the event made a blockade so those fifty people couldn't get near Demi. But on the other side of the car and sidewalk, there was nobody waiting to meet her. So, then as soon as the car door opened, I stood about five feet away and I asked her if I could take a picture with her. She looked at me and said, "Come here, sweetie!" I got my picture with Demi and I was on cloud nine because she looked flawless and beautiful. Even the large crowd of people on the opposite side of the sidewalk was complimenting Demi's beauty. The best part is when I was

Here I am photographed with Demi Lovato in June 2014.

taking the picture so many people were screaming my name in disgust because

I was the only person who got a picture with her. My friend Ron told me about this incident, "sorry about their luck!" because no one of them got a picture with her.

After this experience with Demi Lovato, my admiration for her has only gone up even more. She continues to carry such positive messages for society and mainly for her fans to follow that are just so inspirational to see.

Here I am photographed with Demi Lovato in August 2014.

Pray to Saint Anthony

I was on the subway with my friend Nevin in New York City when he revealed to me that he had lost his wallet and couldn't find it. He didn't tell me about it until this current moment because it was towards the end of the night and he didn't want it to get in the way of our meet up. I have to give props to Nevin for keeping his positivity up during a time of crisis. So, I told Nevin that he should pray to Saint Anthony and that there's a good chance that his wallet will randomly pop back up again. The next morning, I get a message of overwhelming joy from Nevin stating that he found his wallet. The funny part here is that the wallet didn't even leave his vicinity and was in his back pocket of his pants. He told me that because of me and his prayer to Saint Anthony that he needs to become more religious. This was just beyond hysterical and it was just a blessing from Saint Anthony to help him get his wallet back in great and safe condition.

The Selfie King

For those who follow James Franco on Instagram or saw him at the stage door for *Of Mice and Men*, meeting fans you can pretty much say that he is the king of selfies. The best part is that he has even confirmed this through many of his posts on Instagram, as well. However, aside from being the king of selfies, I consider James Franco to be one of my favorite entertainers for the amount of various yet extraordinary projects he takes part in.

What many may or may not know about James Franco is that he is a film teacher at schools in both Los Angeles and New York sharing his appreciation, knowledge, and expertise for film, directing, and acting. What I love about this is that he is willing to share his incredible amount of knowledge in regards to film and share it with those trying to pursue forward in the film industry. It is just great to see and that is why James Franco is one of the most talented yet humble entertainers around.

Here I am photographed with James Franco in August 2014.

For James Franco, when he was starring in Broadway's recent revival, *Of Mice and Men*, he did his very best of putting on a remarkable performance every time he got on the stage. He didn't fail to disappoint while portraying the role of George Milton. But, aside from his acting in the show, the best part of seeing James Franco in the Broadway flesh was how he would sign as many autographs as he could. But, after signing as many pieces as he possibly could accommodate, he would try to take a selfie with them in addition to giving them an autograph. He would then have everyone turn towards the opposite way with his or her front camera on so he can look in and pose for pictures with everyone. Sometimes, for those who couldn't comprehend what to do, he would just position the phone for them and snap the photo.

As it can be seen, James Franco is a highly talented entertainer who just continues to improve and increase the talent in the film industry, but then also ensures that he gives his fans what they want of both an autograph and photo. With his knowledge of taking a selfie with a fan or for his Instagram, there is no question as to why he is considered to be the selfie king.

Here I am photographed with James Franco in June 2014.

Watch GTV Reality

Whether you catch the highly respected paparazzi and collector of entertainment memorabilia, Gio, in the middle of the city or watching his You Tube videos of his encounters with many celebrities, you will just grow a love for his entertaining self. The great lesson from Gio that many need to learn is to just do what makes you happy and have fun doing it. With, Gio's famed slogan, "Stay Black" and screaming or saying multiple times, "Yeah!" you know that you are in for a treat of entertainment and tons of laughter.

The one You Tube video that Gio posted under his nick name, GTV Reality, was an encounter that he had with Alec Baldwin when he was dealing with accusations of being a racist, which were never true to begin with. Gio called Alec his brother, and first questioned the multi-award winning entertainer, as to why anyone would ask if he was a racist because he is the "blackest" guy around. Alec didn't answer so then Gio asked him if he was staying black, and like myself, Alec just started cracking up hysterically in front of Gio.

It can be rightfully admitted that Gio is one of the funniest yet entertaining people around that you can ever meet. And if you haven't watched Gio's videos yet or seen him in person, you are missing out on the Kevin Hart that we have out here in Manhattan.

Here I am photographed with my friend, Gio, also known as **GTV Reality,** in September 2014.

Soul Power Brothers

The pop-rock band that I just find to be so highly talented and inspirational is a band that goes by the name of Emblem 3. The band consists of two brothers named Wesley and Keaton Stromberg who are both originally from California. The irony of two of their song titles that goes by the names of, "Sunset Boulevard" and "I Love LA," which easily intertwines their musical talent and their origination of residency.

Here I am photographed with Emblem 3 members, Keaton and Wesley Stromberg in August 2014.

Emblem 3 emerged on to the entertainment scene when they auditioned for the television show, "The X Factor" and auditioned their own personal song "Sunset Boulevard," in which they wrote on their own and created the sound to. Usually on the "X Factor," the entertainers trying out only tend to do instrumental cover songs and not original songs. I just admire how the Stromberg's felt so comfortable with their own song to do and successfully go on to please the judges of the show. But, because of their confidence with their song and music, they have busted out on to the scene selling out large venues and gaining tons of success by the day.

I had the privilege of meeting both Wesley and Keaton Stromberg this past summer and it was an honor because I enjoy all of their work and I believe they are loaded with so much talent. They both came over to me and greeted me with such generosity and kindness. They were both so willing to sign my stuff that I had related to them while I got individual posed photographs with both Wesley and Keaton. But, my main goal was to get a posed photograph with both of the highly talented Stromberg brothers. Their security guard yelled at me and told me it couldn't happen, but then both Wesley and Keaton said to him, "No it is cool, let him get a picture with us." Some girl grabbed my camera to capture the moment with one of my favorite bands consisting of these two extraordinarily talented brothers.

With Emblem 3's confidence and kindness, they will be selling out venues and tons of music for years to come. If in doubt or struggling with an audition process, take a lesson from Wesley and Keaton Stromberg.

ABOUT THE AUTHOR

The author of this new short story book, "Where Am I Going," Brian Pechar resides in New York where he loves the atmosphere up there. This is Brian's second book consisting of short, positive, and uplifting stories detailing on many experiences he has with others and the World. Brian envisions on writing many more short story books, but also wants to branch out his horizons and work on other projects, as well.

11342033R00031

Printed in Great Britain
by Amazon.co.uk, Ltd.,
Marston Gate.